Bible Stories
for the
40 DAYS

Melissa Musick Nussbaum, storyteller

Judy Jarrett, artist

THIS BOOK BELONGS TO

AND WAS FIRST READ IN THE YEAR

To Abram
    Elisabeth
    Mary Margaret
    Anna Kate and
    Andrew:

You "are a miracle like daily light, As warm, as moving as that luminous air."

Quote above is from "American Child," a poem by Paul Engle.

The author is grateful to Peter Mazar for developing *Forty Days and Forty Nights: A Lenten Ark Moving toward Easter,* which was the inspiration for this book. Thanks again to Peter Mazar and to Theresa Kubasak Turner for reading and critiquing early drafts of the stories, and thanks to Sr. Barbara Bowe for further critique from a scripture scholar's perspective.

Excerpts from the English translation of the Canticle of Moses and Miriam, the Canticle of Hannah and the Canticle of Shadrach, Meshach and Abednego from the *Liturgical Psalter,* © 1994 International Committee on English in the Liturgy, Inc. (ICEL). All rights reserved.

Gabe Huck was the editor of this book, and Deborah Bogaert was the production editor. Anna Manhart designed the book, and Jim Mellody-Pizzato was the production artist who set the type in Veljovic, Motion and Futura. Printed by Thiessen Printing Corp. of Chicago, Illinois.

Library of Congress Catalog Card Number: 97-70097

ISBN 1-56854-179-1

ARKBK

02 01 00 99 98 97   10 9 8 7 6 5 4 3 2 1

LITURGY
TRAINING
PUBLICATIONS

A Note to the Reader

The Bible is a big collection of little books. Some are law books. Some are poetry books. There are books that are letters, like the ones Paul wrote. Some books are filled with wise old sayings, and some are dire forecasts about the end times.

But the Bible is above all a book of stories. And these stories are what Jews first and then Christians have been telling one generation to the next for centuries. These stories are not first of all for reading. They are for telling. They are not silent words on paper. They are sounds in the mouths of Jews and Christians.

They are the stories of people who loved the spoken word: stories told at night around the fire, stories told by grandparents to a new generation, stories told and pulled apart and argued back and forth by people who knew the stories backward and forward. All those storytellers and grandparents and scholars did a great thing: They kept the stories alive and took out meaning and put meaning in.

Now the stories belong to us — for a while. Soon they will belong to our children, and then to their children.

Much changes on our earth and in our lives, but old stories endure. What keeps people talking about Sarah and Abraham, David, Judith, Shadrach and Esther? Why care about ancient dreams, murders and miracles?

To start with, these are just good stories. That alone would keep people telling them. And like all good stories, they need to be heard over and over because the teller and the listener will keep finding something more, something that wasn't there the last time.

But also, these stories taken together tell us what's been going on between God and our people. The news isn't always encouraging, but it's all interesting. The characters in our stories come in every variety of the human condition. We have the harsh story of the near sacrifice of Isaac, the wild love of Rachel and Jacob, the quiet heroics of Esther. These are stories about what happens in this tribe of ours. Even now. Even here.

In this book are stories for each day of Lent from Ash Wednesday to Holy Thursday. Many of them are the stories the church has told for centuries during the days of Lent. Spending the Forty Days of Lent with these stories is a way to move through this time. It is a way to travel steadily toward the great festival of Easter.

But during Lent is only one way to read this book. It can be opened at any time to read a favorite story or learn a new one.

In the book of Deuteronomy, God tells the people:

**Keep these words
that I am commanding you today
in your heart.
Recite them to your children
and talk about them
when you are at home
and when you are away,
when you lie down
and when you rise.**

May the stories in this book lead us all to such love for God's word.

— Gabe Huck

Contents

God Creates One Person, Then Another

God created the heavens and the earth. But the newborn earth looked nothing like it does now. There were no bushes or flowers or grasses or plants of any kind. No wheat grew on the plains. No strawberries flowered wild in the mountains. No potatoes sprouted in the dark soil. For there were no men and women to care for the earth. There were no people to spread seed. There were no children to pick ripe berries from their hidden places or heavy red tomatoes from their groaning stalks.

So God bent down and scooped up some dust from the ground. God made a person from the soil. God fashioned the person like a sculptor working with clay. Head and arms and heart and mind, God made a living being, a human being. From the ground to be tended, God made this first human. When the body was complete, God bent over and blew into the new nostrils the breath of life. Here was one creature made in God's very own likeness.

But there was only one person, and this newly made person was lonely. There were animals of every sort running about the earth, and each was beautiful in its own way. Still, not one of them was human. Not one of them could be a companion for the first and only person.

God saw that such loneliness wouldn't do. So God waited until the new human was asleep. Then God took a rib from the side of the sleeping human and fashioned from the one, another. Partners and companions, God made them. In God's own image, God made them.

A woman and a man, God made them.

And they found in one another an end to the loneliness. They loved each other!

Then God planted a garden in a land called Eden. God welcomed the woman, whom we call Eve, and the man, whom we call Adam, into the garden. God asked them to name every creature in the garden. Every wild beast and every bird of heaven, the cattle and the fish—the man and the woman named them all.

Then they lived with the animals in the garden. Like the animals, Adam and Eve went about naked. And like the animals, these two knew no shame.

Adam and Eve in the Garden

Eve and Adam lived in a green garden, a garden we call Eden. It was filled with flowers and fruit trees. They never had to plant or water or weed. Hail never spoiled their tomatoes. God planted the garden for them, sending just the right amount of sun and rain upon the earth. Like very young children who don't know the difference, Adam and Eve went about naked. They slept when they were tired, picked fruit to eat when they were hungry and played all day long.

One animal in the garden was more clever than all the rest. This was the serpent. The serpent was not happy with the peace of the garden — too boring! So one day the serpent asked Eve, "Is it true that God told you not to eat from any of the trees in the garden?"

It was not true, and Eve said so. "There is only one tree we may not touch," she said, "but we have so many others!"

"Yes," the serpent replied, "but do you know why God has forbidden that tree to you?" The serpent could see that Eve was curious. "God has forbidden that tree alone because it is a special tree. If you eat of the fruit of that tree, you will become like God. You will know what God knows. You will have the power of God to know good and to know evil!"

Eve and Adam, who was standing with her, were pretty happy with the power and knowledge God had given them. But they never knew that there might be more knowledge and more power to be had. The more they looked at the fruit on the forbidden tree, and the more they thought about its being forbidden, the brighter and juicier and more fragrant the fruit seemed to grow. They plucked the fruit and began to eat.

With each bite, Adam and Eve discovered new things. They discovered they were naked. They discovered that their nakedness was embarrassing. They discovered the need for clothes. Worse, they discovered how it felt to disobey God, and in their shame and sorrow, they hid in the bushes.

Now God enjoyed spending time with Eve and Adam. But on that day, **when God came walking in the garden,** Adam and Eve stayed hidden in the bushes. God called out their names. They shouted back, "We can't come out! We're naked!"

"Who told you that you were naked?" God asked, though God already knew the answer. God knew that Adam and Eve had eaten from the forbidden tree. Adam blamed Eve. "She tricked me!" he cried. Eve blamed the serpent. "The serpent tricked me!" she cried.

God would have none of this finger-pointing. God told Adam and Eve they would have to leave the garden. God told them they would have to work hard in order to stay alive. They would have to plant their own garden.

But God never stopped loving Eve and Adam. Even in their disobedience, God had mercy on them. God saw their embarrassment and made clothes out of animal skins for the shame-faced woman and her unhappy partner. The leather clothes must have seemed heavy to people who were used to going about naked, but they were grateful to be covered.

So Adam and Eve left the garden and went out into the world to make their way. They would always long for life in the garden, as we do even to this day.

Abel and Cain

Once Adam and Eve had disobeyed God, trouble spread. When Adam and Eve had children, two sons they called Cain and Abel, there was plenty of trouble. Cain hated his brother!

Abel was a shepherd and Cain was a farmer. Both Cain and Abel brought offerings to God. Abel brought the first-born of his sheep, and Cain brought fruits and vegetables he had raised. God, who knew the hearts of the brothers, was pleased with Abel but displeased with Cain. It wasn't the sheep or fruit that mattered to God. God was concerned with what was in the heart of the one making the offering.

Cain grew angry and more jealous of his brother. He had worked as hard as Abel! Cain thought: "God loves Abel better than me!" Cain was hurt and wanted to hurt God back. He could not hurt God, but he could hurt his brother. So Cain made a plan and invited Abel to go out into the countryside with him. There, away from the eyes of his family, Cain killed Abel. It was the first murder.

Cain's family could not see the killing, but God could see. God called to Cain,

"Where is your brother, Abel?"

Cain replied, "I do not know. And why should I know? Am I my brother's keeper?"

God said, "Cain, what have you done? Listen. You can hear your brother's blood, calling out to me from the ground." God told Cain he had to leave the family.

Cain did not want to leave his home. He did not want to wander the earth. He was afraid that someone would kill him in return for killing Abel. He cried to God, "My punishment is greater than I can bear!"

God had mercy on Cain and placed a mark upon his forehead. The mark was a sign that Cain was not to be killed. He was not to be treated as he had treated his brother.

So Cain left his family and settled alone in the land of Nod, east of Eden.

Noah's Family in the Flood

Abel's murder brought more murder, until God was sorry ever to have created people. So God decided to rid the earth of all people and even the animals, all that God had made and had declared good. But the goodness of one person changed God's mind. That good person was Noah.

Noah walked in peace with all people, and Noah walked in joy with God. God told Noah to protect himself and his family from the destruction God had planned. God told Noah: "Build a big boat, an ark, of wood coated with tar to make it waterproof." God was going to make a flood, a flood such as no one had ever seen before, a flood such as no one would ever see again. Most people and animals would die in the flood, but God had plans for Noah, his wife and their children, and two of every kind of animal. They would ride out the flood in this big ark.

Noah and his family went to work on the ark. They built it, stocked it with food, and rounded up a male and a female of every animal God had made. What a time they had! Children don't eat what penguins eat, and penguins don't eat what orangutans

eat, and how did poor Noah even know what fleas or peacocks or boa constrictors eat? He had to find out, and quickly.

But Noah did all that God asked, and the ark was full when the rain began to fall. It rained for 40 days and 40 nights. Water covered the earth, and Noah's ark sailed upon the waters. The water rose higher and higher, until the tallest mountain peaks were submerged and no dry land could be seen.

God had not forgotten Noah. After those 40 days, God sent a drying wind across the earth, and the waters began to recede. One day, Noah opened a porthole and released a dove into the air. The dove flew out but soon returned. There was no place for the dove to perch, nothing for the dove to eat. Seven days later, Noah released the dove again.

The dove was gone all day, and when she came back in the evening, she had an olive branch in her beak. Somewhere, a tree was peeking above the water! Seven days later, Noah released the dove again. He waited and waited, but she never returned. She had found a dry place to nest. And that's how Noah knew the time had come to leave the ark.

When Noah and his family and all the animals walked out on dry ground, they were filled with gladness. Noah built an altar and knelt down to worship God. God looked upon Noah with love and made a promise to him. God said:

Never again will I destroy every living thing.
As long as the earth lasts,
sowing and reaping, cold and heat,
summer and winter, day and night,
shall never cease.

As a sign of God's promise, a rainbow appeared in the sky. "This," God said to Noah as Noah gazed at the rainbow, "is the sign of the promise I have made to every living thing that is found on the earth."

The Tower at Babel

Noah's grandchildren and great-grandchildren all spoke the same language. That was everyone on earth! If someone meant to agree with a companion, she didn't say "si," while her friend said "oui" or "ja." Grown-ups didn't use one set of words while teenagers used another. If people liked an object, adults didn't say it was "good," while teenagers said it was "cool."

As the people of the earth moved eastward, they found a place on the plains and settled down. There they learned to make bricks and mortar. **"Let's build a tower with bricks and mortar,"** they said, "a tower that will reach all the way to heaven." Perhaps they thought the tower would allow them to climb up into heaven and live there like gods. Perhaps, like Adam and Eve in the garden, they wanted "to become like God."

God saw all that the men and women were doing. Misery and shame came of Adam and Eve's plans. Would misery and shame come of these plans, too? So God decided to end their plans by confusing their language.

All at once, the people could no longer communicate! Some spoke one language, others another. Everyone was talking, and no one could understand. A carpenter might ask for a nail, and his assistant would sing him a lullaby. A painter might ask for a brush, and her partner, not knowing the painter's language, might offer her a loaf of bread.

With such commotion in the community, work on the tower soon stopped. People drifted away. Speakers of one language or another banded together and went off to seek their way in the world. The tower was never built. The town was soon deserted. But first the town got a name we remember to this day. The town was called Babel (like "babble") because there God confused the language of the whole earth.

God calls bram

Sowing and reaping, cold and heat, summer and winter, day and night did not cease. God kept the promise made to Noah. And it came to pass many years later that a child named Abram was born and grew up with his family all around him in a place called Haran.

One day God called to Abram and said, "Leave your country, your family and your parents' house for a land that I will show you." Abram had lived his whole life in Haran! He knew the people there and they knew him. He must have been comfortable in a town so familiar and so dear. Who was this God who could ask Abram to leave his home behind? How could God ask Abram to travel to a land he had never even heard of before? Abram must have been frightened and confused. But Abram listened, and God said more.

God said,

**I will make your children
and your children's children
grow to a multitude.
I will bless you
and make your very name a blessing.
All the tribes of the earth
shall bless themselves by you.**

Abram was probably hoping for directions or an address or a description of the land God promised him! Maybe he wondered how he would earn a living in this land. And we can only imagine the questions Abram's wife, Sarah, had for her husband! But Abram and Sarah trusted God. Though they were old and settled in their home, they trusted God. Though they had only God's word to follow, they trusted and went out as God directed them.

Abram and Sarah, and their nephew, Lot, and all their household left Haran and set off for the land of Canaan. They arrived in Canaan—a long journey south and west of Haran—and settled there.

When Abram was 99 years old, God spoke to him again. God promised children and children's children to Abram, and God gave him a new name: Abraham. The name "Abram" means "exalted ancestor," but the name "Abraham" means "ancestor of a multitude."

Sarah Laughs

Abraham was sitting in the shade by the entrance to the tent where he and Sarah lived in their new land. When he looked up, he saw three strangers standing nearby.

Where Abraham and Sarah lived, noon was too hot to be out in the sun! So Abraham ran out to the strangers to offer them rest in the shade and refreshments. He said, "Please stop here for a while. Relax in the shade of our tree. You can wash the dust of the road from your feet, and then you can have something good to eat."

The strangers gladly sat down in the shade. Abraham went into the tent and told Sarah, "Quick, get the good flour and make rolls for our guests." Next Abraham ran out to the herd of cattle and picked out a tender, choice steer. He gave the animal to a servant for butchering and cooking.

When the rolls were baked and the meat was cooked, Abraham set the table for his guests. While the visitors ate, Abraham waited on them and took care of all their needs.

One of the visitors asked, "Where is your wife? Where is Sarah?"

Abraham answered, "She is in the tent." She was in the tent, and she was listening to everything Abraham and the visitors were saying.

Then one of the visitors said, "I will return next year about this same time. When I come again, you and **Sarah will have a child, a son."**

Now Sarah and Abraham were old. Their hair was white and their skin was wrinkled. Once they had hoped and hoped for a child, but now their time to have children was long past! So when Sarah heard the stranger say she would have a son, she laughed. She did not believe such a thing could happen!

The visitor turned to Abraham and said, "Why is Sarah laughing? Is any work too marvelous for God to do? It will be as I say: When I return next year, you and Sarah will have a son."

Sarah and Abraham did have a son! They named him "Isaac." In their language, "Isaac" means "laughter."

The Binding of saac

Abraham and Sarah must have grown weary trusting God.
God demanded so much! Leave your home, your friends
and your family! Go look for a land only God
knows! Believe that two elderly people
who should have been playing
with their grandchildren would
have a baby! So far, so
good. For all that, nothing
prepared Sarah and

Abraham for what God
would ask next.
God called to Abraham,
and Abraham answered, "Here I am, Lord."
Then God asked the hardest thing of Abraham.
God said, "I want you to take your beloved child, Isaac,
to a mountain I will show you. On that mountain you
must build an altar and there sacrifice Isaac." Abraham could
not understand why God would ask such a terrible thing,
but still he trusted God and prepared to do as God asked.

Early the next morning, Abraham got Isaac out of bed. They said good-bye to Sarah and left for the far-off mountain. They walked for three days. The wood for the sacrifice was tied to Isaac's back. His father carried the fire and the knife.

When they came to the mountaintop, Abraham built an altar. Isaac was confused. Usually his father placed a lamb on the altar and killed it and offered it to God, but no lamb came with them on the journey. Where would his father get a lamb so far from their flocks? "Father," Isaac said, "I see the altar, but where is the lamb for the sacrifice?"

Abraham looked at his son and answered, "Isaac, God will provide the lamb."

Abraham tied up his son and placed him on the altar where the lamb would usually be. Then he raised his knife and held it above Isaac. Just then, an angel of God cried from heaven, "Abraham! Abraham!"

Abraham stopped and answered, "Here I am!"

"Don't hurt Isaac!"

the angel shouted. "It is clear that you love God above everyone and everything. You are willing to offer all that you have to God. God desires that love and willingness. God does not desire human blood."

Abraham looked around and saw a goat caught by its horns in the bushes. He untangled the animal and brought it to the altar, where he sacrificed it in Isaac's place.

A glad and grateful Abraham prepared to go home with Isaac. Before he left, Abraham named the place where he learned what God desires "The Lord Will Provide."

Rebekah at the Well

Abraham was getting very, very old. But he didn't want to die until he saw his son, Isaac, get married. So Abraham called his trusted servant and told him to go back to the land where Sarah and Abraham were born to find a wife for Isaac.

Abraham's servant set out for Haran. When he arrived, he stopped at the spring outside the town. It was evening and time for the women of the town to come and draw water from the well. Abraham's servant had a plan. He would ask one of the young women, "Please give me a drink." If she kindly offered water to him and his camels too, the servant would take this as a sign that she was the one for Isaac.

Just then Rebekah came to the spring to draw water. She was carrying a pitcher on her shoulder, and she was very beautiful. But was she generous to those in need? The servant would find out.

The servant approached her. He asked, "Please, may I have a little water to drink from your pitcher?"

Rebekah quickly lowered the pitcher and offered him a drink. When he had taken enough, she said,

"I'll draw water for your camels, too."

For she saw that they were thirsty.

Drawing water from a well is hard and heavy work, but Rebekah drew pitcher after pitcher until all the camels were refreshed from their journey. Then the man knew: Rebekah was the chosen one.

But Rebekah still had to make her choice. "Do you want to go with this man?" her parents asked her after they had heard about Isaac. "I do," she replied. It was hard for Rebekah's family to see her move so far away. They begged her to stay a while with them, but the servant was anxious to get home. He wanted Abraham to die in peace, knowing that Isaac had found this dear companion. So Rebekah's family said their farewell and blessed her, saying:

> **Sister of ours,**
> **increase to thousands**
> **and tens of thousands!**
> **May your descendants gain possession**
> **of the gates of their enemies.**

Then Rebekah and her servants mounted their camels and followed the servant to the land God had shown Abraham.

While Rebekah and the servant were yet a long way off, Isaac saw them approach. He went out and met Rebekah and heard from the servant of her kindness and hospitality. Isaac married her and found great comfort in her, and she in him.

Abraham's son, Isaac, and Isaac's wife, Rebekah, wanted to have children. But for a long time, no child came. Isaac cried out to God, and God heard. When they had been married 20 years, Rebekah became pregnant with twins.

When the time came for the twins to be born, the first one to emerge was a boy, red-skinned and hairy. He was so hairy he looked as if he were wearing a fur coat. So his parents named him Esau, the Hebrew word for "hairy." His brother was born holding onto hairy Esau's heel, so they named him Jacob, which is close to the Hebrew word for "heel."

Though the boys were twins, they were very different. Esau was a hunter and was happiest outdoors. Jacob liked to stay near the tents which were their home. Their father, Isaac, was glad to have a hunter in the family. Isaac liked to eat the meat Esau brought home, and he and Esau grew very close. But Rebekah preferred Jacob.

One day, Jacob was at home cooking a stew. Esau was out hunting. When Esau got home, he was very hungry. He smelled good things to eat. He said, "Jacob, let me have some of that stew. I'm starving."

Jacob had something Esau wanted: the stew. Esau had something Jacob wanted: the birthright. The birthright was given to the first-born son. It gave him a privileged place within the family and entitled him to a double share in the inheritance that parents left their children. Esau and Jacob were twins, but Esau had been born first, so the birthright belonged to him.

Jacob said, **"I'll give you my stew if you'll give me your birthright."**

Esau said, "Jacob, why are we talking about birthrights? I'm dying of hunger. If I die, the birthright won't do me any good."

Jacob replied, "Swear to me that if I give you this stew, the birthright is mine."

Hungry Esau swore an oath giving up his birthright in exchange for a bowl of Jacob's lentil stew and some bread. Esau ate every bite. When he had finished eating, he went on his way.

Jacob Dreams of the Ladder of Angels

Though Abraham had long ago left Haran, his grandson Jacob went back there to find a wife. But on the way to Haran, Jacob had a strange night.

One day, Jacob was on a long walk. As darkness fell and stars appeared, he stopped to rest. He lay down on the hard ground and propped his head on a stone. A stone pillow—perhaps that is what caused Jacob to have such visions!

Jacob fell asleep and dreamed of a ladder that reached from earth to heaven. The angels of God were climbing up and down the ladder. Still dreaming, Jacob saw God standing beside him. The Lord spoke in Jacob's dream, saying:

I am the God of your ancestors.
Look at the ground on which
you lie: It is yours.
I am giving it to you and your
descendants.
You will have many descendants,
as many as there are grains of sand
upon the seashore.
And I will be with you all:
you and your children
and your children's children.
I will protect you.
If you wander from this land I give you,
I will bring you back.
I will do everything I have promised.

Jacob woke up, and he was afraid. He said, "I simply wanted a place to spend the night, but here I am in the presence of God. I am standing at the very gate of heaven! God is in this place, and I didn't know it!"

Jacob did not sleep much that night. Rising early, he took the stone pillow and set it up as a sacred stone. He poured oil on it and named the place of his dreams and visions Bethel, a Hebrew word meaning "House of God."

Then Jacob made a solemn vow.

"If God will be with me as I was promised in this dream," Jacob said, "I will worship the Lord all the days of my life. I will set this place aside as holy ground, and I will set aside for holy works and worship one-tenth of all God gives me."

Then Jacob went on his way.

Leah and achel

Jacob took a long journey from his home in Beer-sheba to the birthplace of his grandfather Abraham in Haran. But God was with Jacob, and he arrived safely.

Once in Haran, he began to ask if anyone knew his uncle, Laban. The people Jacob asked said that yes, they knew Laban. "Look," they said, "Here comes his daughter, Rachel, with her family's flock."

Jacob walked over and rolled the stone from the mouth of the well so that Rachel could water her sheep. Just then another stone rolled away too: the stone from Jacob's heart. He opened his heart to Rachel at the well, kissing her and weeping for joy. He had found his wife.

But Uncle Laban had two daughters. Rachel was the younger, and the older one was named Leah. Leah had beautiful eyes, but Jacob did not see them. Leah, as the older daughter, was supposed to marry first. But Jacob did not care. He could only see Rachel, whom he loved. Jacob cared only to be with Rachel. He wanted to marry Rachel more than he wanted money. So he proposed to work for Laban for seven years without pay if Laban would agree to their marriage.

Uncle Laban said, "I would be happy if Rachel married a relative of ours. Stay here with us and work."

Jacob worked seven years for Laban. But it didn't seem that long to Jacob, because he loved Rachel. Every day of labor brought him one day nearer to their wedding.

At the end of the seven years, Laban invited people from all around to a feast for the bride and groom.

In those days, brides wore heavy veils, so Jacob could not see his beloved's face at the wedding. After the wedding, night fell, and Jacob still could not see his beloved's face. But when the sun rose and flooded their tent with morning light, Jacob saw that his beloved was not his beloved at all! He had married Rachel's sister, Leah! Laban had tricked him!

An angry Jacob ran to Laban and cried,

"How could you do this to me?" He told Laban,

"You knew I wanted to marry Rachel. We had an agreement. Why did you cheat me?"

Laban said, "In our country, the younger sister cannot marry before the older. Go ahead and have your honeymoon with Leah. After that, I will bless your marriage to Rachel. But," Laban added, "you must give me seven more years of labor."

Jacob agreed. What else could he do? Leah and Jacob had their honeymoon, and then Jacob married Rachel. Jacob loved Rachel so much that he was willing to spend seven more years in Laban's service.

The End of the Many-Colored Coat

God promised Jacob many descendants, and it is true that Jacob and Leah had many children together. But at last Jacob and Rachel had a child. This was Joseph. He was still a baby when some of his brothers and sisters were nearly grown. They resented the love and affection Jacob and Rachel showed this baby brother, the favorite child of the favorite wife. This is what happened to Joseph because of his jealous brothers.

When Joseph's brothers were away tending the sheep, Jacob worried about them. He sent Joseph to see if the young men were well. He told Joseph to bring him news of his sons. The brothers had wandered far from home, and Joseph had to walk a long time to reach them.

Joseph's brothers saw him coming in the distance.

He was wearing a beautiful coat of many colors,

a coat Jacob himself had sewn for Joseph. The brothers were jealous — of Joseph, of his coat, of every kindness Jacob showed him. They plotted to kill Joseph. They planned to throw his body in a deep pit and leave it for hungry animals to find. They agreed on a lie to tell Jacob. "We'll say a wild beast attacked Joseph and ate him up!"

One brother, Reuben, couldn't make up his mind. He didn't want to kill Joseph, but he didn't want to anger his brothers, either. So Reuben made his own plan. He said,

"We don't need to kill him. Just throw Joseph in the pit and leave him there." Reuben and his brothers knew that if Joseph were left in a deep pit, he would starve. If wild animals found him first, he would be eaten. But Reuben intended to return that night and rescue Joseph from the pit. He would send him home to Jacob.

When Joseph found his brothers, they grabbed him, stripped him naked, threw him in the pit and walked away. Some of the brothers noticed a group of traders passing by, going down into Egypt. One of the brothers, Judah, had an idea. He said, "Why should we leave Joseph to die? Let's sell him as a slave to these traders instead. We won't be guilty of murder, but we will be rid of Joseph, and we will have made some money in the bargain." So they sold their brother for twenty pieces of silver, and the traders took Joseph, now a slave, into Egypt.

Reuben came back to rescue Joseph, but the pit was empty. Reuben tore his clothes and wept. Joseph's other brothers did not weep. They did not tear their clothes. They tore Joseph's clothes and dipped the cloth in goats' blood. They took the bloody clothing to Jacob and said, "Do you recognize these?"

Jacob said, "This is my son's robe. He has been attacked and killed by an animal. Joseph has been torn to pieces!" Then Jacob wept. He tore his clothes and mourned Joseph for a long time. Jacob's children, his sons and his daughters, all tried to comfort him, but Jacob would not be comforted. He said, "I will never stop mourning Joseph. I will go down into the grave weeping for him."

But Joseph was not dead. He was in Egypt, where he had been sold to a man named Potiphar, the captain of Pharaoh's guard.

Potiphar's Wife

The traders who bought Joseph from his brothers sold him as a slave to an Egyptian named Potiphar. Potiphar was rich and powerful, and he had an eye for talent. When he saw how skillful and bright Joseph was, he promoted Joseph to be his personal assistant. Joseph took care of all Potiphar's possessions, his house and his business. He did such a good job that the only work left for Potiphar to do was eating! No servant could chew and swallow his food for him!

Now Joseph was as handsome as he was smart, and Potiphar's wife had an eye for beauty. She thought she had fallen in love with Joseph, and she told him so.

Joseph said, "My master trusts me with everything he owns. Though I am a slave, he has made me master of all his possessions. But you are not a possession. You are his wife, and you cannot be with me. How can I act like your husband when you have a husband? That would be wicked, a sin against Potiphar and a sin against God."

Potiphar's wife was used to having her own way. She did not care to be told no. So she waited until she was alone in the house with Joseph, and she grabbed hold of Joseph's clothes and begged him to love her as a husband loves a wife. Joseph again refused her and ran out of the house.

Potiphar's wife was angry. She wanted to punish Joseph. She screamed for

her servants and cried, "Look what this Hebrew has done! He tried to hurt me! But when I yelled for help he ran away! See, here are his clothes. He was undressing when I began to scream."

When Potiphar came home, his wife was waiting. She showed him Joseph's clothes and told him the same lie she had told the servants. Potiphar was furious. He had trusted Joseph! Potiphar called the police, who arrested Joseph and took him to jail.

But God knew the truth. God knew Joseph was not a liar but a faithful and honest man. God stayed with Joseph in prison, watching over him day by day.

Joseph and the Dreams

Joseph was in prison. Two other prisoners there were servants from the household of the Egyptian king, the pharaoh. After they had been in prison some time, the servants both had curious dreams on the same night. They awoke disturbed and wondering. Joseph saw their distress and learned the reason for it. He offered to interpret the dreams, to tell each man what his dream meant. Joseph told them: "One of you will be pardoned by the pharaoh, and the other will be executed by the pharaoh." And Joseph was right!

Two years later, the pharaoh had a dream. He dreamed he was standing by the Nile River, watching seven fat, healthy cows graze in the grass on the riverbank. As the cows grazed, seven thin, unhealthy cows came up out of the river and ate them. The weak devoured the strong, but they were none the stronger for it!

The pharaoh had another dream. He saw seven ears of corn growing on a single stalk. The corn was heavy with kernels, green and full. Behind the healthy corn seven ears of shriveled corn hung

from its stalk. The shriveled corn swallowed up the ripe corn! The pharaoh wanted to know what such visions meant.

The court magicians were summoned. Not one could interpret the pharaoh's dreams. Then the servant who had been imprisoned with Joseph, the one Joseph had predicted would be set free, remembered his jail-mate and his wondrous powers. He told the pharaoh all about the Hebrew prisoner. So the pharaoh called for Joseph.

Joseph was no magician, but God was with Joseph and gave him the meaning of the dreams. Joseph said, "The seven fat cows and the seven ears of ripe corn stand for seven years of plenty. These are the years Egypt is about to enjoy. There will be plenty of rain and sun for the crops and plenty of food for all the people." The pharaoh must have been happy to receive such good news, but Joseph wasn't finished.

He said, "The seven skinny cows and the seven ears of shriveled corn stand for seven years of want. After the years of plenty, the rain will stop falling, the crops will wither and the animals will die. People will go hungry."

Joseph told the pharaoh to pick a wise and honest person to oversee the farms of Egypt. This person must collect all the extra grain during the years of plenty and store it away against the time of want. Only then, Joseph told the pharaoh, would the people of Egypt be saved from ruin.

The pharaoh said,

"Where could I find anyone wiser than you?"

So the pharaoh placed Joseph in charge of the land of Egypt. He had him dressed in fine linen and adorned with gold. He placed the royal ring on Joseph's finger and the royal trust in Joseph's hands. And in all the time he ruled in Egypt, Joseph did not betray the pharaoh's trust.

The Great Family Reunion

The famine came just as Joseph said it would. The famine came to Egypt and spread to the whole world. It spread to Canaan, where Joseph's father, Jacob, and all the family still lived. There was no food to be found anywhere except in Egypt, where Joseph had carefully stored the extra grain from the years of plenty.

When Jacob heard that grain was for sale in Egypt, he sent ten of his sons to buy some. He kept one boy, his youngest son, at home. The boy's name was Benjamin, and his mother was Rachel. So Benjamin and Joseph were full brothers. Jacob feared that something bad would happen to Benjamin on the long trip into Egypt.

Now Joseph was the only one who could order grain to be taken from the warehouses. So when the brothers arrived in Egypt, they came before Joseph and bowed low. They were beggars. If Joseph did not allow them to buy grain, their family would surely die!

The brothers did not recognize Joseph, but Joseph recognized them at once — these jealous brothers who had plotted against him, who had sold him into slavery. Joseph looked at them and remembered the long journey into an unknown land. He remembered his years in prison. He thought of all the nights spent wondering if his father was dead or alive. Would he ever see him again? And now his tormentors stood helpless before him.

Joseph questioned them. When he learned his father Jacob was still alive and that Benjamin was with him, Joseph made a plan. He accused the brothers of being spies. They protested. "We're only here because of the famine! Just sell us food and we will leave!"

Joseph said, "Prove your innocence. Bring your youngest brother here, to Egypt. I will keep one of you in prison until the others return." Heartbroken, the other brothers watched as Simeon was bound and taken away. Weeping, they returned to Canaan.

But they hurried back to Egypt, bringing Benjamin. Now Joseph asked them about their father: "Is he in good health? And is this your youngest brother?" He seemed to be chatting idly with the brothers, but Joseph's heart was full. He turned to Benjamin and said, "May God be gracious to you, my boy." Then he hurried out of the room before anyone could see him crying.

Still the brothers had no idea this was Joseph. So this time, Joseph loaded them down with grain, but he put a silver cup in Benjamin's grain sack. Once Joseph's brothers began their journey home, he sent soldiers after them. The soldiers searched the grain sacks, found the cup, and arrested Benjamin. When the soldiers brought Benjamin before Joseph, his brother Judah stepped forward and pleaded, "If this boy is not with us when we return to our father, he will die of grief.

Please, take me, and let my brother go.

Our father has already lost one son."

When Joseph heard these brave and generous words from his brother, he began to weep again. And now he told them, "I am Joseph, your brother." Such crying and kissing there was in Joseph's house that day! They ate and talked and rejoiced and drank and, no doubt, cried and kissed some more. Then Joseph sent his brothers back to Canaan in wagons piled high with food and money and fine clothes.

They went home to tell their father the glad news that Joseph was alive in Egypt. When Jacob heard, his spirit revived, and he cried, "My son Joseph is alive! I must go and see him before I die!"

So Jacob and every person in his huge family — children, husbands, wives, grandchildren — left Canaan and went to live in Egypt with Joseph. And there they remained for many, many years.

Three Women Save Baby Moses

It wasn't only Joseph's family who came to live in Egypt during the great famine. Many others from Canaan came too. They were welcomed and treated well for a long time.

New pharoahs came and went. Then the day came when a pharaoh who did not remember Joseph came to the throne of Egypt. He looked out and saw all of Jacob's descendants, the great-grandchildren and great-great-grandchildren, and he was afraid. "There are so many of them!" he said. "What if they turn on us? We must protect ourselves against them." So this pharaoh made slaves of all the Hebrews, the descendants of Jacob, who lived in Egypt.

Even as slaves, Jacob's descendants married and had children. Their number grew and grew! So the pharaoh made an evil plan. He ordered the midwives, the women who helped women give birth to their babies in the slave community, to kill every Hebrew boy as soon as he was born. "If there are no boys among the slaves," thought the pharoah, "there will be no soldiers to fight against me." The midwives loved babies, and they worked hard to disobey the pharaoh.

During this time, a certain Hebrew woman, Jochebed, gave birth to a son. She loved her tiny son very much and wanted to protect him from all harm. Jochebed hid the child away for three months. But the baby grew, and his cries were loud, and she couldn't hide him any longer. Soon someone would hear the baby and discover her secret! So she made a basket, lined it with clay and tar to keep out water, and put her baby in the basket. She placed the basket among the tall reeds that grew at the edge of the river. Then she sent her daughter, Miriam, to hide nearby and keep watch over her little brother.

Soon the pharaoh's daughter came down to bathe in the river. She saw the basket in the reeds and looked in.

There was a baby inside! Pharaoh's daughter must have known that the baby was from the slaves, but she didn't care. She picked up the crying baby and comforted him.

Miriam was watching everything. She was wise and brave. She came out of hiding, and though she must have been very frightened, she did not tell any secrets. She knew the lives of many people depended on her! Pretending to be a stranger who had just happened by, Miriam offered to go and find a slave woman to feed and care for the baby. Pharaoh's daughter agreed, and the little girl went quickly off and was soon back with her mother.

Pharaoh's daughter hired Jochebed to care for the baby. She never knew she had hired the baby's mother! So, thinking she had found an abandoned baby, Pharaoh's daughter adopted him. She called him "Moses," a name which means

"I drew him out of the water."

The Burning Bush

Moses grew up as an Egyptian in the pharaoh's own house.
But he always knew he was a Hebrew. Remember that
the woman who cared for baby Moses was his own Hebrew
mother! She surely told him the terrible story of their
people's enslavement by the Egyptians. One day, when he was
a teenager, Moses saw an Egyptian beating a Hebrew slave.
In a fury Moses killed the cruel Egyptian. The pharaoh heard
of the murder and ordered Moses put to death. Moses ran
far away to the land of Midian.

While Moses was in Midian, he got married and began
working for his father-in-law as a shepherd. One day he was out
tending the sheep on Mount Sinai when he saw a strange
sight. A bush was on fire, but it was not burning up! The fire
blazed, yet the bush remained green and whole! Moses
had never seen anything like this. He drew close to the bush.
He heard a voice call his name: "Moses! Moses!"

Moses answered, "Yes, here I am."

The voice said, "Take off your sandals, and come no
nearer. The place where you are standing is holy ground." Moses
took off his sandals and stood very still. The voice said, "I am
the Lord your God. I am the God of Abraham, of Isaac, of Jacob."
Moses listened, but he did not look. He covered his face, for
he was afraid to look at God.

God spoke to Moses: "I see what is happening to the
Hebrews. I hear their cries for mercy, and I mean to save them
from slavery. I want to take them out of Egypt and into a
good land, a land flowing with milk and honey. I want you
to lead the Hebrew slaves out of Egypt!"

First Moses was happy that God wanted to free the slaves.
Then Moses was afraid. He was a wanted man in Egypt! How
could he plead the Hebrews' case before the pharaoh? He had a

good life in Midian. He had not set out looking for God on the mountain. He was looking for the sheep! Besides, Moses knew what a cruel ruler the pharaoh was and how he didn't care who got hurt — or killed! So Moses protested.

"I cannot go alone to Pharaoh!"

God said, "You will not go alone. I will go with you."

So Moses, who had fled Egypt thinking never to return, took courage and made plans to go back to Egypt, the land of his birth.

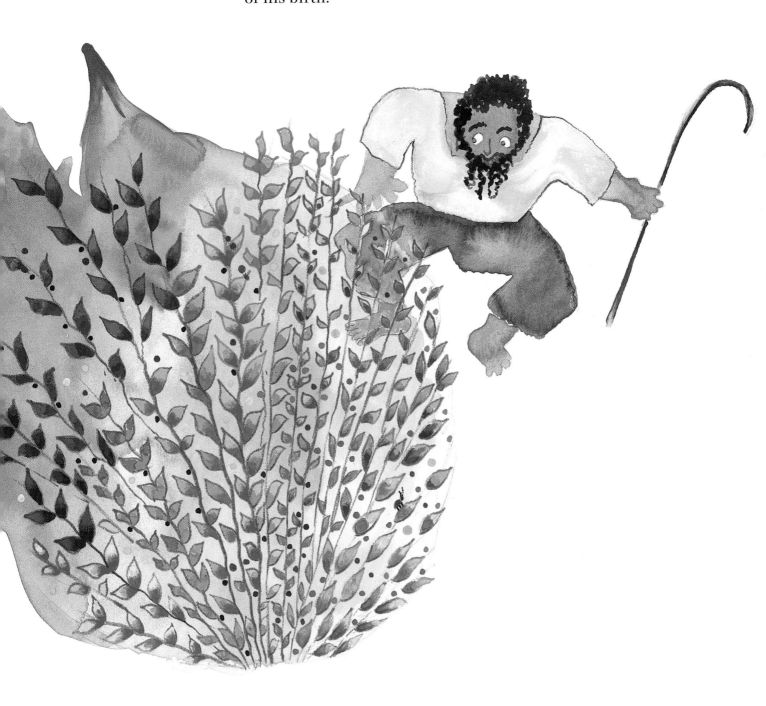

Crossing the Red Sea

Moses did go back to the land of Egypt. He went right up to the palace of the pharaoh and said, "Thus says the Lord, the God of Israel: Let my people go."

The pharaoh said, "What? Who are you? And who is this God of Israel? I do not know this God of Israel. And even if I did, I would not let these slaves go!"

The pharaoh was angry. He decided to punish the Hebrew slaves. He would no longer allow the taskmasters to supply the slaves with straw to make bricks. From now on, the pharaoh ordered, the slaves would have to gather their own straw for the bricks. "But," the pharaoh warned, "each slave has to make just as many bricks as before. They are lazy! If they have more work to do, they will forget this nonsense about freedom!" So life for the Hebrew slaves grew worse and worse.

Because the pharaoh paid no attention to Moses, God sent something he could not ignore: God sent terrible plagues upon the land of Egypt. There were ten plagues in all, each more horrible than the last. Frogs and mosquitoes and locusts swarmed upon the land. Hail hammered the crops into the ground. Livestock died, and the people of Egypt, covered with boils, wished to die. The sun refused to shine.

All of this because God so wanted the slaves to be free! But no one could imagine what it would take to bend the pharaoh's stiff neck.

Then during one long night, the angel of death hovered over Egypt, killing the firstborn of every family, both human and animal. The sound of weeping filled the air. The Hebrews listened to the wails and knew the terrible price of their freedom. God had told them to kill a lamb and mark their doors with the blood of the lamb. The angel of death saw the blood and passed over the houses of the Hebrews. That night, while the Egyptians mourned, the Hebrews followed Moses out of slavery, out of Egypt and into the wilderness.

When the pharaoh, who was crying for his own dead child, realized that the Hebrews had fled, he was angry. He decided there would be more deaths that day if that's what it took to recapture the Hebrew slaves. The pharaoh sent the army after the Hebrews.

Now the soldiers were in chariots pulled by swift horses. The Hebrews were on foot. Before too long, the soldiers caught up with the Hebrews on the banks of the Red Sea. The Hebrews were trapped! Armed soldiers stood behind them. The sea lay before them. They had neither weapons to fight the soldiers nor boats to sail the sea.

God told the Hebrews, **"March on!"**

God told Moses to raise his walking stick and to stretch his hand out over the water. Moses and his followers must have wondered how a raised stick and an outstretched hand were going to make a way through the deep waters. But when Moses did as God instructed, the waters of the sea parted and made high walls on either side of a dry path. The Hebrews walked through the sea!

Then the Egyptian soldiers gave chase, following the Hebrews into the sea. The walls of water flowed in on the soldiers, and they drowned. Soldiers and horses, they all drowned in the sea.

Then Moses' sister Miriam picked up a tambourine, and the people began to dance. They sang:

The Lord is my strength,
the Lord who saves me —
this is the God I praise,
the God of my ancestor.

Quail in the Camp

Moses did what God wanted and led the Hebrew people out of slavery in Egypt into the freedom of the desert. The people were happy to leave. They did not like living as slaves.

The trouble was, they did not like living as free people either. Once, they walked for three days without finding any water to drink! Some of them would have been glad to exchange their freedom for a cool cup of water. They began to grumble.

"We may have been slaves in Egypt," they cried to Moses, "but we were slaves with full stomachs! Now we're free all right, free to starve! It would have been better if God had killed us in Egypt. That would have been easier than slow death in the desert."

God spoke to Moses and told him,

"I will provide food for you."

God said, "I will rain down bread from the heavens. Each day the people are to go out and gather enough for the day."

So Moses assembled the Hebrew people and told them all that God had said. "In the evening," he said, "you will learn who brought you out of slavery. It was God. And in the morning you will see God's glory, for God has heard your cries. Every evening there

will be fresh meat to eat and every morning fresh bread. You can eat as much as you want."

Now the Hebrews had been hunting for food, and they hadn't found a morsel. Where was this feast to be found? That evening, as the sun began to set, the people heard the rustle of wings, hundreds of wings. They looked out and saw the camp filled with quail, birds that are very tasty and good to eat. They caught the quail and roasted them and had a fine dinner.

But the next morning, they woke up hungry and worried again. The ground was wet with dew, and the quail were nowhere to be found. What would they have for breakfast? As they wondered and waited, the coating of dew lifted and revealed a fine powder. It looked like frost, but it was dry. "What is that?" the Hebrews asked.

Moses said, "That is the bread God promised. Take what you need, but only what you need." And the people did as Moses told them. They gathered and ate the bread the way children eat snowflakes that fall gently from the sky. Some people scooped up more and others scooped up less, but when the bread was measured, each person had just the right amount.

The Hebrews ate the promised bread, called manna, for forty years. They ate manna until they reached the land of Canaan. When the Hebrews gathered their first harvest in Canaan, the manna ceased.

Meeting God on Mount Sinai

Three months after they came out of the land of Egypt, the Hebrews reached the wilderness around Mount Sinai. There, in the desert, in the shadow of the mountain where Moses first met God, the Hebrews settled down to wait.

Moses climbed the mountain to God. God reminded Moses of the tender care the Hebrews had known in their flight from Egypt. Like a mother eagle, God had carried and sheltered the people, bringing them safely to the holy mountain. Now God made an agreement, a covenant, with the people. "If you hold fast to my promises and my commands,

you of all peoples shall be my very own,

for all the earth is mine."

Moses returned to the Hebrews and told them all God had said. They listened carefully. Some of them were afraid, because they didn't know what the voice of God might call them to do! They didn't know the rules of the covenant! But they did know the goodness of God. They remembered how it felt to walk safely through the sea on dry ground, and so they answered Moses, "All that God has said, we will do." Moses took their answer back to God.

God told Moses: "Have the people prepare to meet me!" So Moses hurried back to the camp and helped everyone bathe and do their laundry. They scrubbed and cleaned for two days, until on the third day everyone sparkled and shone. At least they thought they did. On the morning of the third day, they saw a radiance that made their own look dim.

For on that morning, thunder rolled and lightning flashed, and trumpets could be heard. The Hebrews trembled as they had trembled before the waters of the Red Sea. Once again, Moses led them. He led them to the foot of the mountain. There they found Mount Sinai wreathed in smoke, for God had descended on the mountain in the form of fire. Fire and smoke reminded no one of the mother-like God who had so far protected and fed them! This was a new and troubling experience of God.

Smoke poured from the mountain like smoke from an erupting volcano. Then the mountain shook as if it too trembled before God. The sound of the trumpets grew louder and louder. Moses spoke, and God answered him with peals of thunder. It was then that God gave the words of the Ten Commandments to Moses.

Deborah, a Judge in Israel

After 40 years in the wilderness, the Hebrews' wandering ended. Their way had been long and difficult. Those who began the journey, Moses and his first followers, did not live to see the journey end. The survivors settled in a land called Canaan. It was the land God had promised them. It was the land to which God had led them.

In Canaan, the Hebrew leaders were called judges. At the time of this story, the chief Hebrew leader was a woman, a judge and prophet named Deborah. (Deborah is a Hebrew name that means "honeybee." We think of bees and honey, but as this story about Deborah reminds us, bees also have stingers.) She lived out in the countryside, in a place now called "Deborah's Palm Tree."

If two people had a quarrel they could not settle, they would come to Deborah's Palm Tree and ask her to decide the dispute. Deborah was so wise, and her wisdom was so well-known, that people agreed to abide by her decisions. Not everyone was happy with Deborah's decisions, but everyone respected her.

Deborah ruled in difficult times. The Hebrews had many enemies. One powerful enemy was King Jabin, who had 900 iron chariots that he used to conquer his enemies and to frighten away those who might become his enemies. King Jabin made life miserable for the Hebrews. But Jabin had not counted on Deborah, who proved stronger than 900 iron chariots and wiser than his most trusted generals.

Weary of King Jabin's oppression, Deborah summoned a Hebrew soldier named Barak and ordered him to raise an army. She told him to lead the army against King Jabin. Deborah believed God wanted her to do this, and so she was not afraid.

But Barak was afraid. Perhaps he had seen all the king's chariots! He said to Deborah, **"I'll go, but only if you go with me."**

Deborah answered him, "All right, I'll go with you." Then she warned him, "But remember this: If I go and we win the battle and conquer King Jabin, the only thing people will remember is that a woman won the day — a woman and not a man!"

Barak's fear of death and defeat was greater than his fear of looking weaker than a woman. So Deborah and Barak went together into battle. They won, just as Deborah had said, and together they sang a song of victory:

"May your friends, O Lord, be like the sun as it rises in its might."

And the land was at peace for 40 years.

The Death of Samson

After the 40 years of Deborah's peace, the Hebrews' troubles began again. The Philistines conquered the Hebrews, who were now known as Israel (the name God gave to their ancestor Jacob). During this time, a baby was born who was named Samson. He would grow up to be a judge in Israel.

Samson the child was not like other children. Samson the man was not like other men. He was so strong that he once ripped apart the jaws of an attacking lion! He was a mighty force for Israel against the Philistines.

The Philistines were desperate to know the secret of Samson's strength. They hired a woman named Delilah to pretend to be Samson's friend. Her job was to get to know all of Samson's secrets. The Philistine leaders promised Delilah a lot of money to betray Samson.

Samson fell in love with Delilah. He did not mind when she asked him the source of his strength, but at first, he teased her. "If I were tied with seven raw-leather bowstrings, I would lose my strength," he said. While he slept, Delilah tied him with seven leather bowstrings and summoned Samson's enemies. But he snapped the bowstrings like cotton thread, and so Samson was not captured.

Then Samson said, "Well, if you tie me with brand-new rope which has never been used, I will lose my strength." Again, Delilah believed him, and again, her plot failed. Samson broke the ropes like spiderwebs.

Delilah got mad. She whined and wheedled every day, bothering Samson so much that he decided to tell her the truth. "I am a Nazirite," he said. "Nazirites make promises to God about how they will live. One of the promises I made is to never, ever cut my hair.

"If I cut my hair, I will lose my strength."

While Samson slept, Delilah cut his hair, and the strength began to leave Samson's body. His enemies came and gouged out his eyes. Then binding the sightless Samson with bronze chains, they led him away to prison.

In prison, no one thought to cut Samson's hair. His sight was gone forever, but his hair—and his strength—were growing.

One day, Samson's enemies made a great feast. They brought Samson out of prison to make fun of him. Samson was led into the banquet hall and placed in the middle, between the two pillars that supported the roof. He could not see, so he asked the boy who was leading him to place his hands against the two pillars.

Samson had a plan!

By this time, thousands of Samson's enemies had crowded into the temple to jeer at him.

As they laughed, Samson prayed for one last burst of strength. He pushed against the temple pillars with all his might. The pillars cracked and the temple roof collapsed. All of Samson's enemies died that day, and Samson died with them.

Naomi and Ruth

Once, during the days when judges like Deborah and Samson ruled in Israel, a great famine came upon the land. The rains did not fall and the crops did not grow, and people had to leave Israel to look for food. A woman named Naomi went with her husband, Elimelech, and their two sons to a land called Moab. Elimelech died in this foreign land.

But soon the family grew again, for Naomi's sons fell in love and married Moabite women. Then suddenly both Naomi's sons died. Naomi the Israelite and her Moabite daughters-in-law, Orpah and Ruth, were alone.

Soon Naomi got news from home that the famine in Israel had ended. She decided to go back to the land of her birth, so the three women set out on their journey.

But as they went, Naomi could not stop worrying about her daughters-in-law. She knew what it was to be a stranger in a land far from home. She knew what it was to have to learn a new language and new customs. Naomi did not want Orpah and Ruth to suffer. She turned to them on the way to Israel and told them to go home. "Go back to your parents," Naomi said, "and may God bless you for your faithfulness to my sons and to me."

"No!" the women cried. **"We want to stay with you. We want to go where you go."**

But Naomi wanted them to go back to Moab. She hoped they would find good husbands there, husbands with whom they could have children.

The three women cried together. Orpah decided Naomi was right. She kissed Naomi and turned back toward home.

But Ruth would not leave Naomi. She said:

I want to go where you go.
I want to live where you live.
Your people will be my people,
and your God will be my God.
I want to die where you die
and be buried there.
Nothing but death can separate us.

So Naomi and Ruth went together to Bethlehem, the town in Israel where Naomi had been born. And there they would remain, for Ruth married a man from Bethlehem. Ruth and her husband, Boaz, became the great-grandparents of David, the boy who would fight Goliath and become a great king in Israel.

Hannah Prays for a Child

During the days of Ruth and Boaz, there lived a woman named Hannah. She was married to Elkanah, who had one other wife. This woman, Peninnah, had children, but Hannah had none. Peninnah used to tease and taunt Hannah. She called her barren, like ground that cannot grow a garden, and made Hannah cry. Hannah felt so sad she could not eat.

Elkanah tried to comfort her. He said, "Hannah, why are you crying? Why won't you eat? How can you be unhappy when I love you so?" But Hannah wanted a child.

Once, Hannah and Peninnah went with Elkanah to the town called Shiloh, to God's temple there. At the temple, Hannah took her stand before God. She was bitter because she could not have children. She was bitter, hurt and angry. Hannah poured out her heart before God. She wept and begged,

"God, listen to me, hear my prayer!

If you will give me a child, I promise to raise that child for you and for your service."

Now Hannah was praying all this quietly. Her words were fierce, but they were uttered under her breath. The priest of the temple, whose name was Eli, watched and tried to listen. But no sound came out of Hannah's mouth. Eli thought Hannah was drunk, and it made him angry to have a drunken woman loitering in the temple, bothering the people at prayer. He said to her, "Sober up! You have no business coming into the temple drunk."

Hannah said, "I'm not drunk. I'm a woman in trouble and I am pouring my troubles out before God."

Eli saw that he was wrong about Hannah. He said, "Hannah, go in peace. May the God of Israel grant what you ask." And Hannah left in peace. Her spirit lifted. Soon she began to eat some food again.

Soon after Hannah and Elkanah got home, Hannah discovered she was pregnant! When a son was born, Hannah named him Samuel, a name that sounds like the Hebrew word for "Asking God," because she had asked God for him. After the baby was born, Hannah used to sing this glad song:

The childless bear many children!
God raises up the poor!

Hannah nursed Samuel until he was ready to be weaned. Then she took little Samuel to Shiloh, to Eli and the temple. Hannah said to Eli, "I am the woman who stood here beside you praying to God. This is the child I prayed for. Now I will honor my promise to God. I've brought Samuel to the temple, and here he will live, serving God every day of his life." Hannah left Samuel with Eli and went alone to pray and sing:

I acclaim the Lord's greatness!
Only you are holy, Lord;
there is none but you,
no other rock like you.

51

The Anointing of Young David

The time of the judges—judges like Samson and Deborah—
ended, and Israel took a king. The first king's name was Saul.
Saul would not live forever, so the day came when God
sent the prophet Samuel, Hannah's son, to look for the next
king of Israel and to anoint the chosen one with oil.

God directed Samuel to a man named Jesse in a town
called Bethlehem, the town where Ruth and Boaz once
lived. In fact, Jesse was Boaz and Ruth's grandson!

God told Samuel that the child who would be king
would be one of Jesse's eight sons. Samuel went as God said.
He first saw Eliab, the oldest of Jesse's sons. Eliab was a
tall, handsome boy. Samuel thought to himself, "Surely God's
anointed one stands before me here!" Samuel thought this
boy looked as a king should. But God doesn't see what we see.
We look at faces and figures, while God looks at the heart.
God said, "Do not judge from his appearance or his lofty stature."
Then God told Samuel to pass Eliab by.

Boy after boy, from Eliab to Abinadab and on down the line, seven of Jesse's eight boys came before Samuel. None was the chosen of God. Samuel must have wondered if he had heard God correctly! He had the horn of oil but no one to anoint. He turned to Jesse, perhaps with some irritation, and asked, "Don't you have any other sons?"

Jesse said, "Well, I do have one other son, the youngest, but he's tending the sheep." Jesse didn't think this little boy of his was a good candidate to be Israel's king!

He was so small!

But Samuel remembered God's warning not to judge by appearances, and someone went and called young David from the pasture. David, though small, was also a handsome boy. Still, he must have been hot and sweaty from his work. His clothes must have been streaked with dirt from the fields and the animals. Yet none of that mattered.

When the boy arrived, Samuel knew. Little David was the one of whom God spoke. Samuel took the horn of fragrant oil and poured it over David's head and all down his body.

Then the spirit of God came upon David and remained with him all the days of his long, exciting life.

A Child Brings Down a Giant

David needed that spirit of God in the hard days that came upon Israel.

While David was still very young, the Philistines declared another war on the Israelites. This time the Philistines had a secret weapon. His name was Goliath, and he was a giant! Goliath was as big as a house and as strong as an elephant. He stood before the frightened Israelites and shouted, "Choose a man to come and fight me! If I win, you will be our slaves. If your man wins, we will be your slaves." The Israelites crouched low in terror. No one volunteered.

Now David was at home still tending the sheep when Goliath challenged Israel. But three of his older brothers were in Israel's army, and David used to go to the front lines to bring them food.

David arrived in the army camp just as the battle was beginning. He ran to the battle lines, looking for his brothers. David heard Goliath come out again and issue his challenge to the frightened Israelite soldiers. David said, "I will fight the Philistine."

King Saul heard David and said, "You cannot go and fight the Philistine! You are only a boy, and Goliath is a man. You have never fought. He has been a warrior all his life."

David said, "I am a boy, but I am also a shepherd. Sometimes lions and bears come to steal my sheep. I have rescued my sheep from the mouths of wild animals. I have fought with lions and bears. I am not afraid to fight Goliath."

King Saul made David put on his own royal armor. Over David's armor Saul buckled his own sword. But when David tried to walk, he found he

could not move! David was not used to so much weight. So he took off the armor and the sword and went out all alone to meet Goliath.

David picked up his shepherd's staff and began to walk toward the giant. On his way, he stooped down and picked up five smooth stones from the river bed. He put the stones in his shepherd's pouch and walked on.

Goliath saw a small boy coming toward him. The boy looked friendly and kind. He did not look like a warrior! He had no sword or spear! He had no servants! Goliath was angry and asked why the Israelites refused to take him seriously. "Do you think I am a dog you can beat off with sticks?" Goliath shouted.

David answered, "You have the strength of your sword and your spear, but **I have the strength of God's name.** Today God will deliver you into my hands. Today all will know that it is God who gives the victory!"

Then David ran toward Goliath. As he ran, David reached into his pouch and took out a stone. He put the rock in his sling and swung the sling round and round. He let the sling go, and the stone flew through the air. The stone hit Goliath on the forehead, and the giant fell down, dead.

The Philistines saw that their champion was dead. They turned and ran. The Israelites ran after them, shouting their war cry all the way. Israel won the battle, and David went to live in the house of the king.

The Queen of Sheba Visits Solomon

King David lived many years. When he died, his son Solomon became king.

Solomon was a wise man, wiser than anyone alive. People brought difficult problems to him, and he solved them. He was also a writer and a musician. Solomon wrote 3,000 proverbs, wise old sayings like:

Go to the ant, you lazybones!
Consider its ways, and be wise.
A little sleep, a little slumber,
a little folding of the hands to rest,
and poverty will come upon you like a robber,
and want, like an armed warrior.

Solomon was well-versed in nature lore. He knew the names of all the trees and flowers and plants that grew in his kingdom. Solomon knew the names and ways of all the birds, fish, reptiles and mammals in his kingdom. Solomon was so learned and so wise that people came from all over the world just to hear him speak.

King Solomon's fame even reached the Queen of Sheba in far-off Arabia. So the Queen of Sheba decided to take a trip to Israel. She would visit Solomon and ask him her most difficult questions. Perhaps she wanted to ask him what stars are made of. Perhaps she wanted to ask him what makes mosquito bites itch. Perhaps she wanted to ask him why ducks don't get cold.

We don't know all her questions, but we do know that she opened her mind freely to Solomon and that he answered all her questions—every one! The Queen of Sheba was delighted with Solomon and pleased by all she saw of his court. The food was good, his servants were polite, and his palace was as fancy and fine as any queen could wish. She said, "The good things I heard about you are all true. How happy your wives (and he had very many) must be! How happy your servants must be! How happy your people must be to listen to your great wisdom!" Then the Queen of Sheba blessed God for giving Israel such a strong and noble king.

It was the custom for kings and queens to exchange gifts. The Queen of Sheba gave King Solomon gold and jewels, and rare and costly spices. She gave him almuggin wood for the temple and the palace. Solomon used some of the almuggin wood to craft harps and other musical instruments. He must have used all the almuggin wood in the world, for none has been seen since the Queen of Sheba visited the King of Israel.

Solomon, who was as polite as he was wise, gave the queen everything she asked for and more besides. Then she and her servants took their presents and went home, back to their own country.

The Widow's Kindness

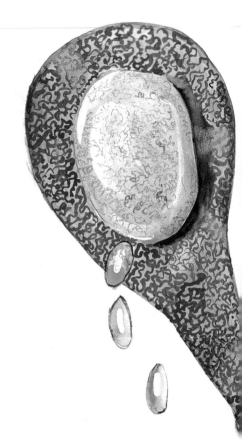

Many years after the death of King Solomon, a man named
Ahab became king of Israel. Ahab was king when God called
Elijah to be a prophet. Elijah knew nothing good would
come of Ahab's rule, nothing good for the people or the animals
or the earth of Israel. Elijah said to Ahab, "There will be a
terrible drought. The rain will stop falling. There will not even
be dew upon the ground." Elijah wanted to warn King Ahab
to stop his evil ways. But Ahab refused to listen.

God told Elijah to leave Israel and flee to the east,
beyond the Jordan River. God directed Elijah to a stream where
the water was sweet and cool. God sent ravens to bring food
for Elijah, and the birds fed him from their beaks. But after a
while, the drought caused the stream to dry up, and Elijah
moved on.

God sent Elijah to a town called Zarephath, to the home of
a widow. Elijah was hungry from his journey, and he asked
the woman for bread. She was hungry herself and said, "I have
no bread. All I have is a spoonful of oil and a handful of
flour. I'm going to make cakes of the oil and flour and cook
them. My son and I will eat this, the last of our food. And
then? We'll just starve to death."

Elijah tried to comfort her, saying, "Do not be afraid."
(Though, of course, she was! It is a fearsome thing to starve to
death and worse to watch a child starve!) And then he told
her, "Go ahead and prepare your meal. Be sure to make some
for me, too."

Now the widow must have thought Elijah a little rude
and pretty stupid. She had just told him there was only a bit of
flour and oil for her and her son. How could she feed three
people when she could not even feed two? How could she feed a
stranger if it meant starving her own son?

But Elijah had gone out into the wilderness without food or water. He knew what it was to wait for God to send ravens to feed him. He knew what it meant to trust in the surprising goodness of God. He said,

Jar of meal shall not be spent,
jug of oil shall not be emptied,
before the day when God sends rain
upon the face of the earth.

Elijah was telling the woman to cook her last bit of food and share it with a stranger. He was telling her to use up all the food she had and believe that more food would be provided. She had to trust. But how could she believe this man? What if he was a liar, a thief who only wanted her last scraps of food?

The woman must have fed Elijah with trembling hands, but she did feed him. She cooked a meal for Elijah, her son and herself. And that meal, which should have been her last, was the first of many, many more. For the jar of flour was never empty from that day forward! The jug of oil was never empty from that day forward! It was all just as Elijah had promised.

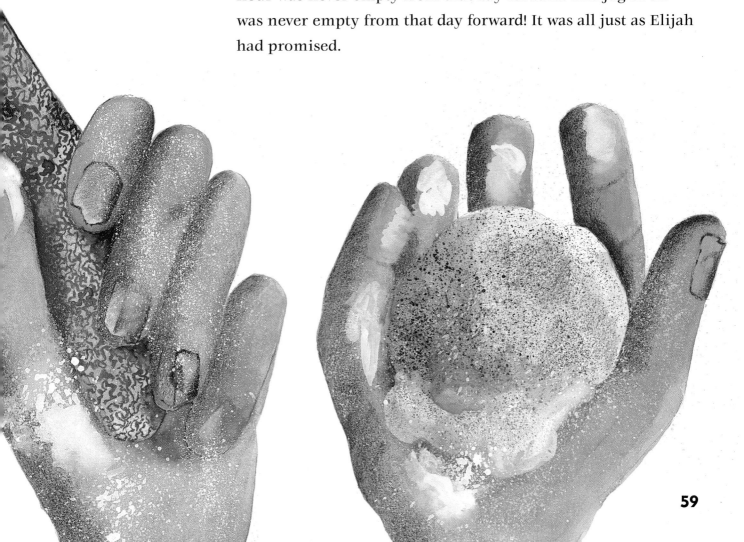

Jonah in the Great Fish

God wanted Jonah to be a prophet. "Get up!" God called to Jonah, "and go to the great city of Nineveh. Tell the people there to turn away from evil."

But Jonah did not want to be a prophet. He did not want to go to Nineveh and tell people news they did not want to hear. He decided to run away. He thought that if he ran far enough and fast enough, God would not find him. To hide from God — that's what Jonah wanted!

Jonah found a ship bound for distant lands. He bought a ticket and got on board. Jonah found himself among sailors from many different lands, each of whom worshiped a different god. When a terrible storm came up and tall waves were sweeping over the boat, the sailors began to pray for deliverance. "Save us! Please save us!" each one called to this or that god.

Now Jonah, who had bigger worries than storms on his mind, had gone below the deck and had fallen fast asleep. Some sailors came for him, crying, "Get up! Pray to your God to deliver us!" They pleaded:

"We don't want to die in this storm!"

But when Jonah said, "I worship the God of Israel who made heaven and earth," the sailors began to wail. They remembered that Jonah was on the boat to escape from this God of Israel! That must be why the winds were howling and the seas were churning! The God of Israel was hunting Jonah down and punishing him with the storm.

"Jonah," the sailors cried, "what should we do? We're all going to die in this storm!"

"It's my fault we're in this storm!" Jonah shouted over the thunder and the crash of waves. "Take me and throw me overboard." The sailors thought about it for a few moments, then apologized to Jonah, wished him well, took hold of him and threw him overboard. At once the sea was calm again.

Even beneath the waves, Jonah could not hide from God. God sent a great fish to swallow him. For three days and three nights, Jonah lived in the belly of the fish. It must have been dark and damp in there, but not as dark and damp as the grave! Jonah was alive! He had been thrown into the raging seas, and God had rescued him. Jonah knelt in the belly of the fish and sang a hymn of praise to God.

**You cast me into the deep,
into the heart of the seas,
and the flood surrounded me.
Deliverance belongs to the Lord!**

God heard Jonah's song and commanded the fish to vomit him up on dry land.

Then Jonah went at last to Nineveh. He told the people to turn away from evil, but he never thought for a minute that they would listen. In fact, Jonah was hoping they would ignore him, and then God would do a spectacular job of destroying Nineveh. Still, the people heard, and they believed in God. Everyone—even the king, even the animals—fasted and prayed. God told Jonah that Nineveh was spared. For God loved Nineveh even if Jonah did not. God loved Nineveh even if the people there did not know their right hands from their left.

61

Jeremiah in the Cistern

In the days of King Zedekiah, the Babylonian army laid siege to Jerusalem, the city where God's temple was and the home of the king. The soldiers surrounded the gates of the city, and the people were afraid.

One of the people in Jerusalem was a prophet named Jeremiah. God had told Jeremiah that Jerusalem would fall. So Jeremiah warned the citizens of Jerusalem to flee the city and surrender to the Babylonian soldiers outside the gates. When the officials of Jerusalem heard what Jeremiah was saying, they grew very angry. "Traitor!" they must have called Jeremiah, and "Turncoat!" "Betrayer of the Jews!" They went to the king and demanded that Jeremiah be stopped.

The king said to them, "You know I am powerless against you. Do what you will."

So the angry men took Jeremiah and threw him into a well. Anyone waiting to hear a splash as Jeremiah hit the water was surely disappointed, for there was no water in the well. The bottom of the well was filled with mud, and into the mud Jeremiah sank.

Now Ebed-melech was a man from Africa who worked in the palace of King Zedekiah. Ebed-melech heard that Jeremiah had been thrown into the well. He ran to the king and pleaded for Jeremiah's life. He said: **"If you leave Jeremiah in the well, he will die."**

The king took pity on the prophet and gave Ebed-melech the order: "Get three helpers and pull Jeremiah out before he dies."

Ebed-melech went to a room in the palace storehouse and found some old rags. He lowered the rags to Jeremiah in the well. Jeremiah, who was no doubt as hungry and cold as he was dirty and damp, must have wondered what good a bunch of rags might be to him!

Then Ebed-melech explained that the rags were for padding. He was going to haul Jeremiah out of the deep well using ropes looped under Jeremiah's arms. The wadded rags would protect his armpits from rope burns. How grateful Jeremiah must have been for the servant's kindness! He was going to be saved, and not only that, Ebed-melech was trying to keep him comfortable in the process!

Then they hauled Jeremiah out of the mud, up out of the well and onto dry land. And Jeremiah the prophet continued to speak God's word. And it always landed him in trouble.

Valley of the Dry Bones

The Babylonians who had surrounded Jerusalem in the days of Jeremiah were triumphant. The citizens of Jerusalem were taken prisoner and sent to far-off Babylon. One of these prisoners was a prophet named Ezekiel.

In Babylon the spirit of God came upon Ezekiel and he was carried off to a valley, a valley filled with bones. Ezekiel walked up and down among the bones. He saw no trees or grass, no flowers or shrubs. Everywhere Ezekiel looked, he saw only bones spread out and piled high, bleached white and dry in the sun.

God asked Ezekiel, "Can these bones live?"

Ezekiel saw only dry bones, dead bones, but he said, "Lord, you know whether they can live."

God said, "Prophesy over these bones. Say, 'Dry bones, hear the word of God. I am going to make breath enter you, and you will live. I am going to put muscle and sinew on you, and you will live. You will learn that I am God.'"

Ezekiel prophesied as God said. While he was speaking, he heard a noise—a rattling, clattering noise. Ezekiel looked around. He saw the bones joining together! Knee bones were finding thigh bones, and thigh bones were joining up with hip bones! Ribs were linking with backbones! Ezekiel watched as muscles and sinews covered the bones! He watched as flesh covered the muscles! But there was still no breath in them.

God said, "Prophesy! Say to the breath, God says this: 'Come from the four winds, breath. Breathe on these dead. Let them live!'"

Ezekiel did as God said. The breath entered them, and the bones came alive! The bones stood on their feet— no longer bones but living, breathing bodies. There were

hundreds of them—thousands! Where before there had been only death, Ezekiel now looked upon a valley filled with life.

Then God spoke again. "Ezekiel," God said, "these bones are the whole house of Israel." The people of Israel, these exiled people living in their enemy's city of Babylon, were sad. They felt as though hope had gone, as though they had died and their bones had all dried out. That's what it was like to be so far from their home, Jerusalem.

So God told Ezekiel to prophesy, and Ezekiel spoke this to the people:

The Lord God says,
O my people,
I am going to open your graves.
I mean to raise you from your graves
and lead you back to the soil of Israel.
And you will know that I am God.
When I put my spirit in you, and you live,
when I bring you home again,
you will know that I have said and done all this.
You will know that it is God who speaks.

Job's Troubles

There was a man in Israel named Job who loved God and turned away from evil. Job had a good life. He had a wife and ten children. He owned thousands of sheep and camels, and hundreds of oxen and donkeys. People all over the land respected Job and honored him.

One day, a council met in heaven. They met with God. One of those at the council was God's rival. God asked the rival, "Where have you been?"

"Round the earth," the rival answered, "roaming about."

God asked if the rival had seen Job in all these travels. God said, "There is no one like my servant Job. He loves God and turns away from evil."

"Well," said God's rival, "why shouldn't Job be good? And grateful, too, while he's at it! Who wouldn't be good if you lavished children and friends and land and wealth upon them?" The rival thought God had spoiled Job! "But," the rival said, "just lay a finger on Job. Take away his children or his possessions, and we'll see if he still loves God and shuns evil."

It was a good question and a good challenge, and God took it. God allowed the rival to take everything from Job, everything but his health. And so it happened. Job's animals were taken—his oxen and camels were stolen, and his sheep were burned alive. This was bad news, but worse news was yet to come. Servants arrived to tell Job that his children had all been killed when their house collapsed on them during a windstorm.

Job rose and tore his clothes and shaved his head, mourning the way people did in his country. Then Job fell to the ground and worshiped God, saying:

**Naked I came from my mother's womb,
naked I will return.
Everything I have God gave me.
It is all God's to give and God's to take.
Blessed be God's name.**

And in all this sadness, Job did not sin, nor did he complain against God.

Once again, a council met in heaven. God asked the rival, "Where have you been?"

"Round the earth," the rival answered, "roaming about."

God asked if the rival had seen Job in all his travels. "There is no one like my servant Job," God said. "He loves God and turns away from evil. His life continues blameless as ever. You tried to ruin him for nothing."

"Skin for skin!" the rival

cried. "It is one thing to touch the people and possessions close to a person, but touch the person's body, and then we shall see! Lay a finger on Job's flesh and bone, and he will curse you to your face."

So God allowed the rival to strike Job's body. God warned: "You must spare Job's life."

Job was struck down with infected sores all over his body, from the top of his head to the soles of his feet. He burned and itched and ached. Nothing relieved his pain.

Job went and sat alone in the garbage dump. He hurt day and night. He said only, "If we are willing to take happiness from God's hand, shouldn't we also be willing to take sorrow, too?" And in all this sadness and pain, Job did not sin.

Job's Questions

Job's friends believed that God was punishing him for his sins. Job said, "No. I have not sinned. I love God and I turn away from evil. I do not know why these terrible things have happened to me and to my family."

Job's friends said, "Only evil people suffer. Good people don't suffer. You must be hiding something from us. Tell us your secret sins."

Job listened to his friends, but he knew he did not have any secret sins. He had only to look around to know that good men and women suffer sometimes, and even children suffer.

Job was so alone. His children were dead. His friends did not believe him. Sometimes Job would weep, and sometimes he would shout at God, asking why such suffering should come.

And once, God tried to answer Job. God's voice was like a great wind, and Job heard God ask a hundred questions:

Where were you when I laid the foundation of the earth?

Where were you when the morning stars sang together and all the heavenly beings shouted for joy?

Where is the way to the dwelling of light, and where is the place of darkness?

Surely you know!

Have you entered the storehouses of the snow?

Can you send forth lightning?

Do you give the horse its might?

Is it by your wisdom that the hawk soars?

Job trembled at all these questions, all these wonders God had done. And Job answered God: **"I have uttered what I did not understand, things too wonderful for me."**

Sometimes Job hurt so much he wanted to die, but Job did not die for a long time. After all his trials, Job lived to be 140 years old. God restored everything that Job had lost. All that was taken, God returned.

Three daughters and seven sons were born to Job after the time of his suffering. Some people in those days valued sons more than daughters. But Job, who had learned much in his pain, valued his daughters as much as his sons. And when he died, an old man and full of days, Job's daughters inherited equally with his sons.

The Fiery Furnace

When Nebuchadnezzar was King of Babylon, he conquered the land of Israel and carried off its treasures. The greatest treasures of Israel were its young people. The brightest and most faithful of them Nebuchadnezzar carried off to the land of Babylon.

The stolen youth promised to remain faithful to the God of Abraham and Sarah, of Rachel and Jacob. They promised to sing God's praises even when the people of Babylon praised other gods.

King Nebuchadnezzar built a great golden statue and called all the people in Babylon to bow down before it and worship. "When you hear the sound of the trumpets, when the flutes and harps begin to play," the king told the people, "fall on your faces and pray." He warned everyone who did not worship the shining statue that they would be burned alive in a fiery furnace.

Some men came to the king and whispered rumors that three young men from Israel named Shadrach, Meshach and Abednego refused to fall down and worship the golden statue. The king was very angry. He did not like to be disobeyed.

Shadrach, Meshach and Abednego were brought before the king. He asked, "Is it true that you do not worship our gods? Because if this is true, you will be thrown into the fiery furnace. **And what god will save you then?**"

Nebuchadnezzar must have expected the young men to weep and beg and promise to do anything—anything!—if only he would save them from the flames. But the three young men were not afraid! They said, "The God we serve is able to save us from the fiery furnace. But even if God chooses not to save us, we will be faithful. We will not worship your gods. We will not bow down before the golden statue."

Nebuchadnezzar grew angrier still. His face was red and twisted with rage. The king ordered the furnace heated seven times hotter than usual. He ordered the three young men bound with ropes and thrown into the roaring fire. The fire was so hot that it roasted the soldiers who threw Shadrach, Meshach and Abednego into the furnace!

Inside the furnace, though, an angel of God blew a coolness like a breeze off the sea. The fire couldn't touch the three young men, and right there in the furnace they started to sing. Now Nebuchadnezzar was astonished, because over the roar of the fire he heard this song:

Bless God, fire and heat.
Give praise and glory.
Bless God, frost and cold.
Give praise and glory.

The king came as near to the fire as he dared and called, "Shadrach, Meshach and Abednego, servants of the Most High God, come out!"

The faithful young men did not crawl out of the furnace gasping for air. For they were not burned! The hairs on their heads were not singed! They didn't even smell of smoke! No, they walked out singing:

God has freed us from the raging flame
and delivered us from the fire.
Give thanks, the Lord is good!
God's mercy endures forever!

And even Nebuchadnezzar joined in singing:

Blessed be the God of Shadrach, Meshach
and Abednego!

Susanna's Trial

This is another story that happened after the people of Israel, the Jews, had been taken to exile in Babylon. They lived there a long time. Some, like Susanna and her husband, Joakim, even settled down in Babylon and prospered.

Susanna was a woman who loved the God of Israel. Her faithfulness shone in her face. Joakim became a rich and respected man. People came to him for advice. Two men who had been chosen as judges among the Jews were frequent visitors to Susanna and Joakim's house. These men appeared to be wise and righteous, but God knew their hearts were evil.

These two men spied on Susanna when she walked in her garden. They were filled with desire for her, both of them wanting to lie with Susanna as a husband lies with a wife. But they did not want to live in trust and devotion with her as a husband lives with a wife. Their intent was only to take what they wanted from her.

They watched and waited, hoping to catch Susanna alone. One hot day, she came out into her garden to bathe alone. She had no idea the evil men were in the garden with her, peering out from their hiding place in the bushes.

The men came out of hiding and said to Susanna, "Do as we tell you. Give us what we want. If you refuse us, we will tell everyone you are seeing a young, handsome man behind your husband's back. And people will believe us. We are important men! Who will believe you?"

Susanna was trapped! "But," she said, "whatever happens, I will not sin against God. If I fall into your power, I will fall innocent of all wrongdoing." And with that, she began to scream for help. Then the men began to scream, too, trying to sound like people who have just come upon a terrible sight. All the commotion aroused the household, and men and women came running to the garden. The evil men told everyone: "We found Susanna in the garden! She was kissing a young man!"

Well, no one thought that sounded a bit like the Susanna they knew, but these men were important men! So a trial was arranged for the next day.

The evil men gave their testimony. "We were walking in the garden," they said, "when a young man came out of hiding. He and Susanna began to kiss and caress like lovers. We witnessed this crime and ran to catch the man, but he got away. We caught her, though!"

Susanna listened to this and turned her eyes to heaven, her heart confident in God. She knew she had done no wrong.

But the people believed the evil men. After all, they were important men! So Susanna was condemned to death, as were all people convicted of adultery in those days. She heard her sentence, and she said:

Eternal God, you know all secrets!
You know these men have lied about me.
Must I, who am innocent, die because of their sin?

God heard Susanna's cry and roused the spirit in a young boy named Daniel. He began to shout, "I will have nothing to do with this woman's death!"

"What do you mean?" the people asked him.

"Are you really so stupid?" Daniel demanded of the people. "You know Susanna. Will you take the word of these men against her without even hearing her side of things?"

That made sense, so the people allowed Daniel to question each man separately. That way, the two men couldn't get together and agree on a lie.

"Now then," Daniel said to the first man, "you say you saw Susanna and a man lying together under a tree."

"Yes, I did," the liar said confidently, for he was accustomed to being believed.

"What kind of tree?" Daniel asked. "A mastic tree," the man said.

Then Daniel went to the second man and asked him the same question. "A holm oak," the wicked man replied.

And so the people knew the truth about Susanna. They cheered Susanna, who had shunned evil and trusted in God. They cheered Daniel, who had done the just work of God. And the people blessed and praised God, who hears the cry of the oppressed.

Daniel in the Lions' Den

Along with Shadrach, Meshach, and Abednego, a young man named Daniel was captured and taken to Babylon to serve the king. Daniel lived a long life there, and he served many kings: first the Babylonian kings, then the Persian kings who conquered Babylon. This story happened when the Persian King Darius sat on the throne of Babylon.

King Darius trusted Daniel and set him over all the princes of the kingdom. Darius believed Daniel had a wonderful spirit, but the other princes saw only Daniel's power, and they were jealous. The princes tried to catch Daniel doing something wrong. But Daniel was faithful, in public and in private, and no one knew of any wrong he had done. So the princes decided to trap Daniel. They worshiped the King of Babylon as a god, but they knew that Daniel worshiped the God of Israel alone.

The jealous princes went to King Darius. "O, King," they said, "live forever! We are all agreed that no one should pray to any god but you." They asked King Darius to write a law ordering punishment for people who pray to any god other than the king. The punishment was harsh: Law-breakers were to be thrown into a den of hungry lions.

Daniel heard of the new law, but he did not stop praying to God. Three times a day he went home and fell on his knees to pray and give thanks to God. The jealous princes snuck around Daniel's house and peered in his windows. What they saw pleased them. Daniel was praying! He had broken the law! They heard him asking the God of Israel for all his needs, and they ran to tell the king.

King Darius was a good person. He did not want Daniel to be eaten by lions. The king thought and thought of a way to set Daniel free. But the law was plain: Daniel had prayed to the God of Israel and not to the King. Daniel had to be thrown to the lions.

Darius was sorrowful and said, "Your God, whom you have served so faithfully, will have to save you." Then the king watched as Daniel was taken to the lions' den. A heavy stone was rolled over the opening of the den. There would be no escape!

The king went home in tears and spent the night waiting and watching. He could not eat, he could not sleep, and no one could comfort him. As the sun rose, Darius ran to the lions' den shouting, "Daniel, Daniel! Was your God able to deliver you from the lions?"

Imagine Darius' surprise and joy when Daniel answered him! Daniel called out from the pit, "God sent an angel to close the lions' jaws!"

Darius ordered that Daniel be released from the lions' den. Darius wrote a decree that everyone in the kingdom should honor the God of Daniel:

The living God endures forever!
God saves and sets free.
God works signs and wonders!
God has saved Daniel from the power of the lions!

Judith Saves Her People

The Jews had just returned from exile in Babylon when another enemy appeared — the Assyrians, led by General Holofernes! The Assyrian soldiers cut off the water supply. If the Jews tried to leave their towns to search for water, the Assyrian soldiers turned them back. People wailed, "God brought us home again only to watch us die of thirst!"

One of the Jews was a woman named Judith. Judith was wise and faithful. She prayed that God would deliver her people from the hands of the Assyrians. When she got up from her knees, Judith knew what she had to do.

Judith bathed and dressed in her finest clothes. Then, calling her maid to come along, Judith set out for the camp of Holofernes. As Judith left the town gates, the elders of the community blessed her, saying:

> **May the God of our ancestors look upon you with favor!**
> **May God fulfill your purposes, to the glory of Israel,**
> **to the glory of Jerusalem!**

They knew that Judith had a courage they did not possess. They stood within the safety of the gates and watched Judith go down the mountain and across the valley until they lost sight of her.

Soon Judith met Assyrian guards. They demanded to know what a Jew was doing so near their camp! Judith told them that she did not want to be with the Jews when the mighty Assyrian army overran their fields and towns! Judith told the soldiers she had secret information for Holofernes.

The soldiers took Judith into the camp. Some of the Assyrians had never seen a Jew. They looked at noble Judith and asked, "Who could despise a people who produce such women?" Judith asked to be allowed to go out each morning to pray and to go out each evening to bathe. This was part of Judith's plan.

Judith had been in the Assyrian camp for three days when General Holofernes asked her to a banquet in his tent. Judith came into the tent, and Holofernes wanted to kiss her. He cried, "Enjoy yourself with us!" and began to drink glass after glass of wine. His soldiers and servants did likewise for fear of offending their master. But Judith was shrewd. She remained sober while Holofernes and his soldiers got very drunk.

It grew late. Holofernes' guests staggered to their own tents and fell asleep. Judith and Holofernes were alone. But Holofernes was too drunk to stay awake. He collapsed, unconscious, on his bed. Judith sat keeping watch.

Near dawn, when all the camp was quiet, Judith stood and began to pray:

Lord God, to whom all strength belongs,
prosper what my hands are now to do.

Then, grabbing Holofernes' sword, she seized him by the hair and cut off his head. Then she tore down the canopy and wrapped Holofernes' body in it. Taking the head, she called for her maid. The maid came and did not scream or cry out, for she was brave like her mistress. The two women put the head into the maid's food sack and walked calmly out of the tent. The two left the camp together, as they always did when they went to pray.

Once Judith and her maid were out of the camp, they made their way back to the territory still held by the Jews. While they were yet a ways off, Judith began shouting,

"Open the gates! God is still with us!"

Everyone, old and young alike, came to the gates to meet her. They threw open the gates, welcoming the brave women. Judith cried out:

Praise God! Praise the God who shows mercy to Israel!
Praise the God who has delivered our enemies into my hands!

With that, Judith opened her bag and pulled out Holofernes' bloody head. She held it up for all to see and said, "God used a woman to strike him down!" The people knew the siege was over. They would have water again. Men and women and children fell to the ground and worshiped God. One of the elders sang: "May you be blessed, my daughter, by God most High." And the people all answered, "Amen! Amen!"

Esther Saves Her People

There once was a king, Ahasuerus, who ruled the lands from India to Ethiopia. His deputy was a man named Haman. Many different peoples lived in Ahasuerus' kingdom, but of all of them, Haman hated only the Jews.

Haman went to the king and said, "There is a certain people living in your kingdom who are not like you and me. They do not keep the laws of our gods, and they do not keep your laws, either. I know that we would be better off without them. With your permission, I will issue a decree calling for their destruction."

Ahasuerus was disturbed at the thought of an alien, lawless people in his kingdom. So he let Haman send letters throughout the land ordering the killing of all the Jews, young and old, women and men and children, too. He ordered that all the Jews be killed in one day!

What neither Haman nor even King Ahasuerus knew was that Ahasuerus' beloved wife, Esther, was a Jew! They didn't know and would never have guessed. Ahasuerus was looking for strange and lawless people. He didn't think Esther was lawless or strange! He loved and admired her.

So Esther was safe with her secret. She didn't have to say a word. No one would harm the queen! Others might die, but Esther would be spared.

Yet when Esther found out about the plan to kill the Jews, she was not willing to keep silent while people died. She made a daring plan. The plan would mean that her own life was at risk, but if she succeeded, the Jews would be saved.

Esther prepared a sumptuous banquet for her husband. She made sure that all his favorite foods were on the table. King Ahasuerus was pleased and touched. Then, after dinner, all at once Esther turned to her husband and said, "There are plans to kill me and all my people. If you care for me, spare my life and the lives of all my people."

Brave Esther did not know what her husband's reaction would be. She must have been frightened as she waited for him to speak! Would he hate her, too, when he learned that she was a Jew?

King Ahasuerus was angry, but not at Esther. He cried, "Who dares to hurt you? Where is this wicked one?"

Esther answered, "It is your deputy, Haman, who is my foe. It is Haman who has told you falsely that every Jew is your enemy." Then she looked at him directly and said:

"And I am a Jew."

So at the last minute, King Ahasuerus stopped the plans to kill the Jews. In every city, on every farm, wherever the Jews lived, there was gladness and rejoicing. The Jews declared a holiday in honor of Esther's great courage, and they keep the festival, called Purim, to this day.

The Bible is filled with stories — scary stories, curious stories, funny stories, joyful stories, wondrous stories. There are stories of brave children and of faithful parents. There are stories of wise rulers and of bold saviors. There are stories of prophets who speak truth and of judges who rule justly.

Now we come to the stories of Jesus. Jesus was a kind and loving person like Ruth, a just judge like Deborah, a good shepherd like David, a suffering prophet like Jeremiah, bold like Esther and full of wisdom like Solomon. All through the year, Sunday after Sunday, we hear the stories of Jesus and of those who came before him in faith. When we meet Jesus as Lent comes to a close and Easter draws near, he is on his way to Jerusalem.

The Stones Would Shout!

Jesus' disciples were with him near Jerusalem. As they walked along, Jesus sent two of the disciples into a village. He told them to find a colt, a young horse, that had never been ridden. They were to find the colt tied up near the entrance to the village, and they were to bring it to Jesus. Jesus told the disciples all they were to say and do.

The disciples did everything that Jesus asked of them. They went into the village and found a colt tied up on the street. They untied the colt and began to lead it away. Some men who lived in the village were watching. They saw strangers come in and untie the colt. But they didn't see the strangers ask anyone to borrow the colt! They didn't see the strangers buy the colt from its owner! They must have thought they were watching some very bold robbers! So the men stepped forward and said, "What are you doing? Why are you taking that colt?" Perhaps they thought the frightened disciples would drop the reins and run. But the disciples were not frightened. Jesus had told them this would happen. The disciples said as they had been instructed, "The Master needs this colt. He will send it back directly." And the men let them go.

The disciples took the colt to Jesus. Then they spread their cloaks on the colt's back and made a kind of soft saddle for Jesus. He sat down, and they all continued on into Jerusalem.

People were watching Jesus from the roadside. They lined up as he rode into Jerusalem. Some spread their cloaks on the ground before Jesus. Others cut down fresh green branches and put them on the ground to make the path smooth and soft for this great procession. The path before Jesus was glorious, covered with the offerings of the men and women who shouted:

Hosanna!
Blessed is the one who comes in the name of the Lord!
Hosanna in the highest!

Some of the people in the crowd said, "Jesus, tell your disciples to stop that kind of talk!"

Jesus answered: **"I tell you, if they were to keep silent, the stones would shout!"**

And in this way, Jesus entered Jerusalem.

A Woman Anoints Jesus for Burial

Now the time was near when Jesus would be arrested and crucified. He and his disciples were staying in Bethany, a little town just east of Jerusalem. One night, they were having dinner together at the house of a man named Simon.

During dinner a woman walked into Simon's house and did an amazing thing. She was carrying a jar made of alabaster, a costly and beautiful stone through which light can shine. The alabaster jar was filled with fragrant oil. It made the whole house smell warm and wonderful. This was an oil carefully prepared to soothe and refresh the skin. Very few people could afford such expensive oil. Those who could probably would use only a few drops at a time, and any sensible person would be very careful of the alabaster jar when measuring out the oil. Both the oil and the jar were precious!

But this woman was not at all sensible. The worth of the oil and the jar didn't seem to matter to her. Instead of pouring out a little oil, she broke the jar and dipped her hands into the oil as it spilled out. Lifting her hands, she let the oil pour on Jesus' hair. She smeared the oil on his face with her fingers.

The other guests were amazed, and some were angry. The angry ones said, "What does she think she's doing? Why, she could have sold that oil for hundreds of dollars! She should have sold it and given the money to the poor! This is a disgrace!" They expected Jesus to agree with them and rebuke her. They knew how much Jesus cared for the poor.

But Jesus said, "Leave her alone! What she has done for me is good." He told them, "The poor you will always have with you, and you can be generous to them day after day after day. But you will not always have me with you. Don't you see what she has done?

By anointing and perfuming my body,
she has prepared it for burial.
Wherever the good news is proclaimed,
what she has done will be told in memory of her.

Jesus Washes Everyone's Feet

After the great entry into Jerusalem, after the wonderful anointing with the sweet-smelling oil, Jesus knew that the time of his suffering had come. He knew the days ahead would be terrible for his mother and his friends, who loved him. This is the story of what Jesus did to show how much he loved them.

Jesus and his friends were at supper. All at once he got up from the table and wrapped a towel around his waist as a servant would do. The disciples must have wondered why their master was dressing up like their servant!

Then Jesus took a basin and filled it with water. He went to each person there, one by one. In front of each person, he put down the basin of water. Then he knelt and bent over and began to wash and dry their feet. Now these feet must have been very smelly! People in those days wore sandals and walked long ways on dirt roads. It was a kind and gracious thing to wash the tired, dirty feet of one's guests. But it was not something the host or hostess would ever do. Washing feet was unpleasant work — servant's work!

So when Jesus came to Simon Peter, the disciple stopped him. "Lord," he said, "are you going to wash my feet?" He did not like what he was seeing.

Jesus said, "At the moment you do not understand what I am doing, but later you will understand."

Simon Peter said, "No! You shall never wash my feet!"

Jesus answered him, saying, "Simon Peter, if I do not wash your feet, you cannot be my companion; you will have no part in me."

This alarmed Simon Peter, who loved Jesus. He said, "Lord, then wash my feet and my hands and my head as well!"

When Jesus had finished washing everyone's feet, he sat again at the table. He said, "Do you understand what I have done? You call me Master and Lord, and it is right for you to do so. If I, your Master and Lord, wash your feet,

then you must wash one another's feet.

I have given you an example. Do for one another what I have done for you."

Then they sang songs and psalms.

Judas eaves

One of Jesus' disciples was named Judas Iscariot. He came to supper and sat while Jesus washed his feet. He sat while Jesus told the disciples to wash one another's feet. But he was not listening to Jesus. Instead, he was filled with anger and hatred.

Jesus knew that one of the disciples, one of those who walked and talked and prayed and ate with him, was going to turn him in to his enemies. It hurt to know that a close friend would do this, would hand him over for trial. Jesus looked sorrowfully around the table and said, "I tell you most solemnly, one of you will betray me."

Simon Peter was confused. How could anyone here betray Jesus? He looked around and saw that one of the disciples was sitting very close to Jesus with his head on Jesus' chest. This disciple nestled against Jesus like a frightened child in a parent's arms. Simon Peter caught the eye of this person and gestured in a way that meant, "Ask! Ask Jesus who will betray him."

So the disciple asked,

"Who is it, Lord?"

"It is the one," Jesus replied, "to whom I give the piece of bread that I shall dip in this dish." He dipped the bread and gave it to Judas Iscariot. Judas took the bread, and Jesus said, "What you are going to do, do quickly."

No one at the table understood what was happening between Jesus and Judas. They all knew that Judas took care of their money, so some of them thought Jesus was telling Judas to go out and buy what was needed for the Passover feast. Some thought Jesus was telling Judas to go give money to the poor. But Judas knew, and Jesus knew. As soon as Judas took the bread, he went out.

Night had fallen.

eter Gets Scared

After Judas left, Jesus turned to the others and began to speak. He told them, "My children, I am not to be with you much longer." And then he said:

> **I give you a new commandment:**
> **Love one another.**
> **Such as my love has been for you,**
> **so must your love be for each other.**
> **This is how all will know you for my disciples:**
> **by your love for one another.**

Peter heard only Jesus' words that he was leaving. He said, "Lord, where do you mean to go?"

Jesus answered, "I am going where you cannot follow me now. Later on you shall come after me."

Peter was hurt and confused. He cried, "Lord, why can I not follow you now? I will lay down my life for you!"

Jesus turned to Peter and said, "You will lay down your life for me? I tell you truly, the cock will not crow before you have three times disowned me."

It was all true, all of it. Judas turned Jesus over to his enemies. Jesus was arrested and taken to court. Peter saw everything that happened, but he never came forward to stand with Jesus.

Peter waited in the courtyard of the place where Jesus was being held. It was night, and it was cold. Peter stood before an open fire, warming his hands. A servant recognized him. She said, "Are you not one of this man's followers?"

"Not I!" Peter replied.

Others recognized Peter too, and asked, "Are you not a disciple of Jesus?" Peter denied it and said, # "I am not!"

But one of the servants insisted, "Did I not see you with Jesus in the garden?" Peter denied it again.

At that moment a cock began to crow.

And so it happened just as Jesus said. Peter heard the cock crow, and he remembered what he had said to Jesus and what Jesus had said to him. Peter went away crying.

But Jesus also had said that Peter would someday come after him. For though Peter denied Jesus, Jesus never denied Peter. The day came when Peter proclaimed Jesus as Lord before the multitudes. From that day forward, Peter was never again ashamed or afraid to be known as a follower of Jesus. Peter followed Jesus, and he was faithful in life and in death.

Prayers for the Three Days

Lent ends on Holy Thursday in the evening. All of us enter the Three Days, the Triduum. We fast and pray and watch and wait through Good Friday and Holy Saturday. Then in the night between Saturday and Sunday, we come together for the Easter Vigil. On Sunday we end our Triduum and begin the Fifty Days of Easter.

The Triduum has its own stories, which Christians tell when they gather on Good Friday and at the long Vigil. Along with these stories, the Three Days have songs and prayers like these.

From Holy Thursday night until Easter Sunday:

We should glory in the cross of our Lord Jesus Christ,
our salvation, our life, and our resurrection.
In Christ we are saved and made free.

On Holy Thursday night:

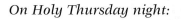

The Lord Jesus,
when he had eaten with his disciples,
poured water into a basin
and began to wash their feet, saying:
"This example I leave you.
If I, your Lord and Teacher, have washed your feet,
then surely you must wash one another's feet."

On Good Friday:

Holy is God!
Holy and strong!
Holy immortal One, have mercy on us!

We worship you, Lord,
we venerate your cross,
we praise your resurrection.
Through the cross you brought joy to the world.

On Holy Saturday:

Christ our Lord,
like the seed buried in the ground,
you brought forth for us the harvest of grace.

At the Easter Vigil:

This is the night
when first you set the children of Israel free.
You saved our ancestors from slavery in Egypt
and led them dry-shod through the sea.

O truly blessed night!
Heaven is wedded to earth!

On Easter Sunday:

Alleluia! Alleluia! Alleluia!

Map of the Holy Land

Haran •

Euphrates River

→ Nineveh

Cyprus

Mediterranean Sea

Syria

• Damascus

• Zarephath

Israel

Sea of Galilee

Jordan R.

Babel (Babylon) →

Canaan

• Shiloh

• Bethel

Jerusalem • • Bethany

• Bethlehem

Moab

Arabian Desert

Beer-sheba •

Dead Sea

Egypt

Nile River

AFRICA

Red Sea

Midian

Mt. Sinai (Horeb)

Ethiopia ↓

India →